A PORTFOL

# HOME
# ENTERTAINMENT
# IDEAS

COWLES
Creative Publishing

# CONTENTS

© Copyright 1998
Cowles Creative Publishing, Inc.
5900 Green Oak Drive
Minnetonka, Minnesota 55343
1-800-328-3895

Printed in U.S.A.
Library of Congress
Cataloging-in-Publication Data
A portfolio of home entertainment ideas.
      p. cm.
   ISBN 0-86573-891-2
   1. Recreation rooms--United States. 2. Interior decoration-
-United States--History--20th century. 3. Home entertainment
systems--United States.     I. Cowles Creative Publishing.
NK2117.R4P67  1998
643'.55--dc21                                      98-7293

Associate Creative Director: Tim Himsel
Editorial Director: Bryan Trandem
Managing Editor: Jennifer Caliandro
Project Manager: Michelle Skudlarek
Writer: Carol Harvatin
Editor: Clayton Bennett
Art Director: Kari Johnston
Copy Editor: Janice Cauley
Vice President of Development
Planning & Production: Jim Bindas
Production Manager: Patt Sizer

Printed on American paper by R. R. Donnelley & Sons Co.

COWLES
Creative Publishing, Inc.
Minnetonka, Minnesota, USA

President: Iain Macfarlane
Group Director, Book Development: Zoe Graul
Creative Director: Lisa Rosenthal
Senior Managing Editor: Elaine Perry

## Other Portfolio of Ideas books include:

A Portfolio of Kitchen Ideas

A Portfolio of Deck Ideas

A Portfolio of Landscape Ideas

A Portfolio of Bathroom Ideas

A Portfolio of Window & Window Treatment Ideas

A Portfolio of Flooring Ideas

A Portfolio of Bedroom Ideas

A Portfolio of Unique Deck Ideas

A Portfolio of Lighting Ideas

A Portfolio of Water Garden & Specialty Landscape Ideas

A Portfolio of Porch & Patio Ideas

A Portfolio of Storage Ideas

A Portfolio of Fireplace Ideas

A Portfolio of Ceramic & Natural Tile Ideas

A Portfolio of Fence & Gate Ideas

A Portfolio of Outdoor Furnishing Ideas

A Portfolio of Home Spa Ideas

Photos on page two (top to bottom) courtesy of KraftMaid
Cabinetry, Inc.; Milling Road, A Division of Baker Furniture; and
Valley Recreation Products. Photos on page three (top to bottom)
courtesy of First Impressions Design & Management, Inc.;
Vidikron; and interlübke.

Photos on cover (clockwise) courtesy of The Franklin Mint;
Sub-Zero Freezer Co., Inc.; Bartley Antique Reproduction
Furniture Kits; interlübke; and Brunswick Billiards.

Photo courtesy of Milling Road, A Division of Baker Furniture

# WHAT MAKES A GREAT ENTERTAINMENT AREA?

Today's home entertainment areas look nothing like the family parlors of years ago. Our ideas about family fun have changed and so have the rooms we use for recreation. These days, the money required to set up a home entertainment area that includes a home theater or full-size pool table should be considered an investment in a family lifestyle.

An entertainment area can be a vital part of your home—a room that's more casual than the living room and more functional for social and family gatherings than the kitchen. An entertainment area can be a place where the kids can get together with friends to play table tennis or just a comfortable place where you can relax and enjoy a good movie complete with surround-sound. A well-planned entertainment area does all this and more. All you need to create a great entertainment area is an understanding of the activities you want to do there and the atmosphere you want to enjoy while doing them.

*A Portfolio of Home Entertainment Ideas* provides many ideas for room arrangements, all chosen to get you thinking about the

possibilities for your own home entertainment area. Large, color photographs detail a variety of popular items often included in entertainment areas. You'll find suggestions for selecting the design elements that will help you create the atmosphere you want.

This book begins with suggestions for planning, along with examples of different design elements, such as room size, furniture, storage, lighting, aesthetics and acoustics, and appliances and accessories that can enhance your enjoyment.

The next part of the book is divided in two sections—one that focuses on home theater systems and one that features parlor games and indoor sports, such as billiards, darts and table soccer.

*A Portfolio of Home Entertainment Ideas* will inspire you with ideas to help you make the most comfortable, functional entertainment area possible with the space you have. You'll find plenty of inspiration and hundreds of ideas that can be adapted to create a functional, comfortable, customized entertainment area that reflects the leisure activities you enjoy most.

Photo courtesy of Audio Design Associates, Inc., photography by Phillip Ennis

**Formal traditional** *meets high-tech modern in this room. A formal, elegant sitting room is transformed into a comfortable theater for watching sporting events and films, through the use of a projection television and pull-down viewing screen. Modern electronic equipment stored in traditional glass-faced cabinets with interior lighting creates an interesting style juxtaposition. When not in use, the screen is retracted to reveal a traditional piece of artwork.*

# Planning Your Entertainment Area

Begin planning your entertainment space by thinking about who will use the area and what activities they will want to enjoy. Do you want an area primarily for home theater use? A parlor theme, with gaming tables, darts and bumper pool? A full-featured, multifunctional area? Consider all your family members, friends and neighbors, and the activities you might want to enjoy with them in your home entertainment area.

Once you've determined the activities you want to include in your entertainment area, you need to choose some specific elements to include. Your decision depends on whether you want to create a home theater or a gaming parlor. With a little creativity, you may be able to develop an area that's a combination of both. The primary element you include, like a front-projection-screen television, pool table or dartboard, becomes the focal point of your home entertainment area—the single item that the rest of the room is designed around.

Primary elements can be grouped into three types: *sound systems,* *home theater systems* and *indoor sports and parlor games.* Within these three groups, there are a variety of different items you may want to consider. Later in this book, you'll get a closer look at some of the most popular primary elements, and learn how to choose which ones would work best for your family's entertainment area.

After you've chosen the primary elements you want to include, it's time to assess the design features that will help you enjoy those elements. We have divided the design elements into six groups—*room size, furniture, storage, lighting, aesthetics and acoustics* and *accessories and appliances.* Each of these elements helps enhance your enjoyment of the entertainment area. When planning your space, think about each primary element and how it relates to the six design groups.

Photos courtesy of Milling Road, A Division of Baker Furniture

(above) **Cabinet entertainment centers** *are a good choice for smaller spaces, because they can organize many features in a small area. In rooms that see a variety of functions, an entertainment cabinet can effectively hide and protect electronic components when they're not being used.*

(left) **Large entertainment features***, like a billiards table, dominate the space they occupy. Since these are permanent fixtures, make sure to choose styles that are appealing to you; you'll be living with your choice for many years. Such large features usually require a dedicated space, though a billiards table can sometimes be integrated into a very large multifunctional entertainment area.*

7

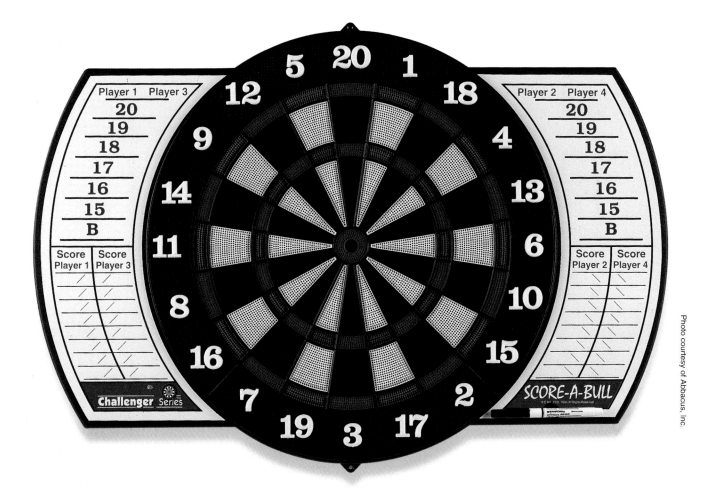

Player 1    Player 3
20
19
18
17
16
15
B

Score   Score
Player 1  Player 3

Challenger Series

Player 2    Player 4
20
19
18
17
16
15
B

Score   Score
Player 2  Player 4

SCORE-A-BULL

Photo courtesy of Abbacus, Inc.

PLANNING

# PRIMARY ELEMENTS

The primary elements featured in this book are by no means the only options available; they simply reflect the most common and popular items included in today's home entertainment areas.

Home electronics includes all types of stereo and surround-sound systems, television sets, videocassette recorders (VCRs), laser-disc players, digital videodisc players (DVDs), big-screen TVs, home theater systems, projection screens, satellite dish and cable components.

Another primary element is indoor sports, such as pool, bumper pool, table tennis, darts, table soccer and air hockey. For less physical gaming, there are specially designed tables that let you play board games, like cribbage and chess, and card games, like poker and bridge. Some gaming tables are available in

octagonal shapes that can accommodate as many as eight players.

Indoor sports and gaming are popular elements for home entertainment areas, but need careful planning. Some activities take up more space than others, and most require room for participants and viewers to move around.

The last primary element, food and drink, can be part of the activity no matter what else is going on. Whether you're staging a world premiere in your home theater, holding an indoor sports tournament, listening to new releases on your sound system or getting together with friends for an evening of cards, most everyone will want refreshments. Be sure to think about what food and drinks you want to serve in your home entertainment area, and plan to include space for preparing, serving and cleaning up.

Photo courtesy of Irwin Seating Company, Inc.

**A top-end home entertainment feature** is the complete home theater, featuring a projection television unit, large reflective screen and theater seating. A surprising number of homeowners are opting for such luxury elements these days, but home theaters on a more modest scale are even more popular—and more affordable. Home theaters are especially well suited for basement expansions, where there are few windows.

Photos courtesy of Roche-Bobois

# DESIGN ELEMENTS

In this book, we're using the term design elements to describe the features in a room that enhance the enjoyment you and your guests get from your home entertainment area. Design elements can be divided into six basic groups:

**Room size.** This plays a large part in determining the activities you will be able to include in your home entertainment area. For example, room size determines whether you can include a pool table and is an important factor in planning a home theater area as well.

**Furniture.** Your needs change as the room's function changes. Think of the activities that will take place most often in the area, and choose the furniture you'll need for those activities. Carefully measure any components you plan to put on shelves or in cabinets to make sure the spaces are large enough to hold the components. Other furniture items you may want for your entertainment area include: tables, stools, benches, bars and serving carts. A variety of materials work well for furniture in home entertainment areas; some of the most common and durable frame materials are wood and metal.

Seating in entertainment areas can include any of several options, from simple bar stools to luxury lounge sofas. Again, your planned activities will determine the best furniture choices for your space. If you want an entertainment area that provides a complete home theater experience, you will probably want to include large, comfortable chairs or couches that are conducive to watching a screen for long periods. Other seating options include a wide selection of chairs, bar stools and benches. Large, comfortable captain's chairs that swivel and roll on casters are ideal for seating around a gaming table. Overstuffed couches and chairs are comfortable for long periods of sitting.

You'll also need tables, countertops or bar-top areas to set glasses and dishes on. Popular table options for entertainment areas include gaming tables in octagon shapes that accommodate up to eight players, wet or dry bars and standard tables in various sizes and shapes.

The cabinets and bookcases that work best for entertainment areas have doors that close to hide a TV screen and other electronic elements that can make a room look messy or cluttered. Make sure the doors swing completely out of the way or slide easily back into the cabinet so the screen is unobstructed. Cabinets with doors will also protect electronic equipment from dust. Cabinets should also have proper circulation throughout to keep your equipment from heating up. Make sure the cabinetry you choose leaves enough room for wires; some cabinets have built-in cord-minder features that collect and hold cords. This makes upgrading the system in the future much easier.

**Furniture sets the style** for your entire entertainment area. In this room, all furniture elements have smooth, rounded features to create an ultramodern look. The choice of light wood tones and warm colors creates a relaxed environment. Like all good home theater cabinets, the cabinet shown here has doors that close to conceal the television when not in use (opposite page).

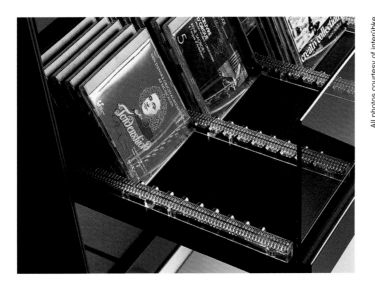

## DESIGN ELEMENTS

**Storage.** The furniture you choose for your entertainment area should be able to hold all your necessary accessories—television, videocassette recorder, digital videodisc player, etc. The sizes of electronic items vary widely, so measure everything before investing in a cabinet. Buy shelves with as much adjustability as possible so there will be room later for new equipment and storage for videotapes, discs and video games. Your entertainment area should also include storage for any other necessary items, like board games, books, pool cues, darts, dishes and serving trays.

***This attractive low-profile entertainment cabinet*** *can hold a television, a VCR and a complete stereo system. Slide-out racks conveniently store videotapes and compact discs (opposite page). Although traditional-style cabinets often seek to hide the electronic components, modern-style cabinets like this one often openly display the television and stereo equipment, using them as design elements to emphasize the high-tech style of the room.*

*Wall-mounted track lighting is ideal for illuminating works of art, such as paintings or photographs. Track lighting provides great flexibility and can also be used to create mood lighting or general room illumination.*

*Variable-color light fixtures let you adapt the lighting to match your mood of the moment. This high-tech lamp has colored filters and a variable control that can create any color you want.*

*Modern light fixtures are chosen as much for their design appeal as for the illumination they provide. This fixture is programmable to create entertaining lighting effects that constantly change.*

## DESIGN ELEMENTS

**Lighting.** The lighting needs of a home entertainment area will depend on the activities that will take place. Gaming tables require the broad, even lighting provided by large overhead fixtures hanging directly above the table. On the other hand, home theaters have very different lighting needs. Adjustable, indirect lights are ideal for ambient lighting in home theaters. They provide a soft, indirect, adjustable light source that won't interfere with your viewing.

Home listening areas are designed primarily for sound, but even here the lighting is important. You will need to have enough light to use your sound system easily, but will probably want to vary the lighting to suit the mood of your music. Ambient light from sconces and torchères with dimmer controls are popular for listening areas.

Proper lighting ensures the best viewing conditions for any activity, from watching

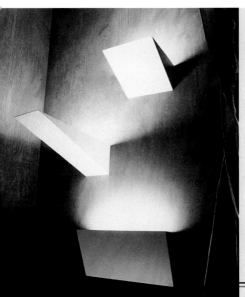

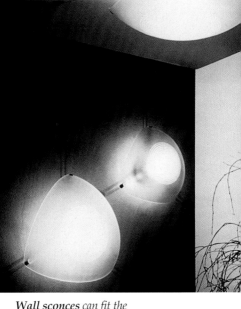

*"Light wedges"* mounted on the wall not only illuminate the room, but provide a bold geometric design element. Obviously, such fixtures work best in a room with a modern, high-tech decor.

*Some light fixtures* are quite literally works of art—created by world-renowned designers and sculptors. Like any work of art, limited-edition lighting fixtures can become highly prized collector pieces.

*Wall sconces* can fit the style of any decor, from traditional to ultramodern. Sconces are best suited for providing accent light and diffused general illumination. The model shown here uses halogen bulbs for maximum brightness.

movies to playing board games. Still other areas and activities have different lighting needs. Desk lamps are helpful for computer workstations, whether the computer is being used for work or play.

While the lighting for your entertainment area should be flexible enough to accommodate a variety of activities, remember that lighting also helps create the atmosphere for your home entertainment area. For decorative effects, recessed ceiling spot lights and track lights can be used to highlight the dramatic elements in a room. You may choose accent lights to show off your game room artwork or collection of antique sporting goods. Track lights and uplights (floor spots) are ideal for drawing attention to these kinds of displays. And sometimes a light source is a decorative item in itself, as with neon signs or a jukebox.

Photo courtesy of U. Schaerer Sons Inc./HALLER SYSTEMS™

Photo courtesy of Broyhill Furniture Industries, Inc.

## DESIGN ELEMENTS

**Aesthetics and acoustics.** These elements enhance the visual and aural comfort in a room. The aesthetic ingredients of an entertainment area can include color and materials for floors, walls and ceilings that are decorative and durable. Window treatments should complement the decorative style of the room. If your entertainment area is decorated to look like an old-fashioned poolroom, your window treatments should match the decor. If your space has the contemporary feel of a modern movie theater, your choice of window treatment will be quite different.

The acoustic needs of your home entertainment area will vary from one activity to another. Acoustics will determine the best positioning of several items—starting with your speakers, especially if you have a surround sound system. To create a sense of being in the middle of the action when you watch movies, you can bounce the sound from your center speaker off the walls of your entertainment area. On the other hand, if you are listening to the delicate sounds of a classical orchestra, you probably want the clearest, cleanest sound possible.

**Appliances and accessories.** These help you store, prepare and serve food and drinks. Appliances and accessories in entertainment areas are primarily used for food and drink preparation and do not really change from one activity to another. Appliances such as refrigerators, microwave ovens, can openers and ice makers all help you prepare snacks and drinks—which remain the same whether you're playing table soccer or watching the Super Bowl.

***The mood and tone*** *of your entertainment spaces will be determined by the style of the elements you include. A sleek modern style (opposite page) can be achieved by including elements that use modern materials: steel, glass and laminates in sharply geometric shapes. Electronic equipment, such as a stereo, may be openly displayed as a design element. A traditional style, on the other hand, calls for natural woods and textiles (above) and heavier, more substantial shapes. In traditional-style spaces, it's usually best to hide the electronic components in cabinetry.*

# HOME ELECTRONICS

At the heart of many entertainment areas lie high-tech electronics—stereo sound systems with tape decks and CD players, big-screen televisions with surround-sound and satellite reception, laser-disc players, video games, VCRs and DVD (digital videodisc) players. Each of these components is available in a variety of models and styles with numerous feature options.

The home electronics system you choose should depend on the function you want it to serve. If you plan to use your stereo sound system primarily to provide background music for other activities, you will probably be happy with a boom box or a mini system that will be easier to use and less expensive than a component system. On the other hand, if you have a passion for listening to classical music on high-quality digital recordings, you should invest in components that are sold separately. For the true audiophile, buying high-quality speakers is a good investment.

In most homes, a television set is at the center of home entertainment. With so many programs available through broadcast, cable and satellite, television provides something for everyone in the family. In addition to regular programming, a television offers opportunities for playing back movies on tape or disc, showing home videos and playing video games. The best television set in the house is usually placed in the most comfortable room, with plenty of seating for family members and friends.

*Serious hobbyists often devote an entire room to one theme. State-of-the-art audio equipment forms the heart of this entertainment space. The electronic gear is displayed openly and proudly, and the entire room decor is aimed at providing a comfortable listening experience.*

*A home theater can be as elaborate as you want to make it. Here, an entire room has been given over to a home theater featuring a large screen, a ceiling-mounted projection television and large, comfortable seating. Reflective "stars" on the ceiling, mock pillars and cinematic wall hangings transport viewers into a world of imagination.*

# STANDARD TELEVISIONS

The choice of a television set is important for the success of most home entertainment spaces. The typical small television set is not very well suited to a true home entertainment experience. Many small sets, those with screen sizes of 13 to 20 inches, are regarded as "second sets" by manufacturers, who tend to make them with monophonic sound, few extra features and limited options.

Mid-size sets, those with 25- to 27-inch screens, are considered the minimum standard for full-featured home entertainment areas. These sets usually offer more features, such as picture-in-picture, special sound systems and universal remote controls. "Comb filters," which allow a TV set to produce greater detail, are commonplace on 27-inch sets but are not found on most 25-inch models.

New technology has created dramatic changes in television. One of the most recent is the merging of TV and video functions with those of computers to produce new multimedia products like WebTV. Introduced by Philips and Sony, WebTV provides access to the World Wide Web without using a desktop computer. Instead, you connect an Internet terminal (a box the size of a small VCR) to a television set.

When you choose a television for your home entertainment area, look primarily for picture and sound quality, price and repair history. And make sure the model you buy will fit into whatever cabinetry you are planning to use.

(left) **A small television** mounted in a cabinet is a good addition to a kitchen or informal dining area.

(below) **A large standard television** can be placed in a wall cabinet unit designed for the purpose. This wall unit also holds a complete surround-sound stereo system, with speakers hidden by fabric-covered cabinet doors. Wall units should have good ventilation to prevent the television from overheating.

# BIG-SCREEN TVS

Big screens aren't just about picture quality; they're about creating the ambience of a big theater experience. Direct-view big screens range from 34 to 40 inches. Direct-views have the same basic technology as standard televisions, using cathode ray picture tubes (they're sometimes referred to as CRT TVs). The larger the screen, the larger and heavier the tube must be. The weight and size of this style can be too much for many shelving units, so check on this before making a purchase.

Televisions larger than 40 inches use projection technology, in which the image is projected onto a reflective screen—either from the rear or from the front. Projection sets can offer picture areas as large as 80 diagonal inches, but the picture quality is usually inferior to that found on conventional picture tubes.

On some models, the thin reflective screen is attached to a wall, while in others, the screen pulls down from the ceiling for convenient storage. Most large direct-view sets and projection sets come with plenty of features, such as ambient sound and custom settings.

Big-screen projection televisions require big spaces. With front projection TVs, you need to sit well back from the screen to ensure a sharp image —at least 8 feet away for a 40-inch screen, and as much as 20 feet away for an ultralarge 80-inch screen. Brightness and color start to vary if you move to either side, so you'll need to configure furniture so you sit directly in line with the screen.

In smaller spaces, it's best to go with the large direct-view TV rather than a projection model. But if you have a large room that you plan to dedicate to a home theater—and a budget to match—a projection television can create a unique viewing experience.

Photo courtesy of Room & Board

**Home theaters can be portable.** *This big-screen direct-view television has been mounted in a sturdy rolling unit that can be moved around at will. This may be a good option for small or medium-size multipurpose rooms, where a permanent home theater configuration isn't practical.*

*(left)* **Corner cabinets** *can be the best solution for positioning a large direct-view television in a cramped space. Several manufacturers offer such cabinets.*

*(below)* **In a large room,** *a big direct-view television can be integrated into cabinetry that covers an entire wall. When buying a big-screen television, check its overall dimensions to make sure it will fit into the cabinetry you have in mind.*

Photo courtesy of Broyhill Furniture Industries, Inc.

# VCRs & DVDs

Although laser discs have a small share of the market, videocassette recorders (VCRs) are the most popular format for playing commercial movies at home. Better models have stereophonic sound that will record and play back high-quality sound, including the surround-sound that many movies feature. High-band VCRs offer excellent picture quality and special effects; some even have editing features. However, these high-tech units also require expensive tapes that can be hard to find.

Because programming a VCR is still a mystery to many, VCR makers keep trying to simplify the task. VCR Plus+ is a feature built into many models that does the programming for you; it allows you to use the remote to enter a program code found in the TV listings of newspapers. With that code, VCR Plus+ automatically switches to the channel you want to record at the right time.

When choosing a VCR for your home entertainment area, look for these key features:
• *Auto channel set* programs the VCR to recognize only the channels containing a broadcasting signal and to ignore channels that do not.
• *Auto clock set* uses information in the broadcast signal to set the clock on the VCR unit. This eliminates the flashing "12:00" that occurs whenever the power is interrupted.
• *Auto rewind* automatically rewinds the tape when it reaches the end.
• *Cable channel capacity* indicates the number of separate signals the VCR can receive.

A new device for playing movies at home is the digital videodisc (DVD) player. Featuring the latest technology to reach the home theater market, these players use discs that are compatible with both home video systems and personal computers. DVDs are smaller and less expensive than full-size laser discs. Movies on DVD appear sharper than videotapes and sound much better, especially in six-channel Dolby digital surround-sound. A special kind of receiver is necessary to take advantage of all the new features of DVDs, but the results are impressive. For those who have already invested in full-size laser discs, combination machines are available that play both laser discs and DVDs.

Digital videodiscs are similar to compact discs (CDs) and compact disc–read only memory (CD-ROM) media, but can hold as much as 20 times more data. As computers become more prominent in home entertainment, thanks to their sophisticated video functions and game-playing abilities, expect DVD to be an important medium for both computer and home theater use.

**Most television cabinet units** *have compartments that will hold a VCR or DVD player, as well as other electronic equipment. Additional shelves and drawers hold videotapes, discs, video games and other accessories.*

Photo courtesy of Milling Road, A Division of Baker Furniture

Photos courtesy of Room & Board

**This oak television cabinet** *fits nicely into a modern or country setting and is perfect for smaller rooms where space is important. The doors close to hide the television and accessories used for viewing.*

25

# HOME STEREO SYSTEMS

Stereo sound systems are available in a wide range of styles, from simple boom boxes to elaborate configurations combining a half-dozen or more separate components. The system you choose will depend on the way you intend to use the equipment and on the quality of sound you want.

The most flexible (and costly) stereo systems are component systems. Component systems allow you to include only the pieces you want and upgrade them whenever you like. They also provide the best sound quality, provided you choose the right combination of elements. Check the compatibility of components before investing in them. Some combinations work better than others, and some don't work at all.

Rack systems are full-size, prepackaged home stereo systems with the components already matched. Like component systems, rack systems require assembly. The units must be wired together, and the outer cabinets must be put together. Although rack systems come with full-size speakers designed to stand on

the floor, speaker stands are available to enhance their sound.

A dual cassette deck, CD player and remote control are standard features on most rack systems. More expensive models include home-theater features, like Dolby surround capabilities. In general, the best rack systems will match the performance and versatility of a good component system, but at a lower price. Some manufacturers cut costs by using cheaper cabinets, typically made of laminated particle-board with thin back panels.

A mini system is a small, all-inclusive stereo system that comes as one complete unit. Mini systems are popular because they're cheaper, more compact and simpler to set up than separate components. One drawback to mini systems is that they can't be upgraded with bigger speakers or other components. They also usually lack adjustable bass and treble controls.

When the quality of a sound system is not critical to the enjoyment of music, a simple boom box is acceptable. Boom boxes combine an

*Many stereo listening systems are now designed to accept input from your television, providing much better sound than the built-in TV speakers. In this setup, the electronic components are openly displayed on stylish open shelving units.*

AM/FM stereo radio, built-in antenna, one or two cassette decks, and a CD player in one portable package. Boom boxes can be run on household current or batteries. Some have detachable speakers that can be positioned for a better stereo effect. The more expensive models even have remote controls.

*(right)* **This component system** *finds a home on a sleek storage unit with glass shelves.*

*(below)* **For many people,** *a stereo system is the most important—and in some cases the only—home entertainment element.*

# SURROUND-SOUND SYSTEMS

Traditional stereo sound systems, which have just two channels of sound, are gradually being displaced by surround-sound systems, which feature as many as six separate channels of sound. A modern surround-sound stereo system can incorporate all the standard input devices—CD player, cassette deck, FM radio tuner and even a traditional phonograph. When listening to music, surround-sound gives the illusion of being inside a concert hall. But unlike many two-channel stereos, a surround-sound system can handle the sound from your television set, making true home theater a practical option.

Surround-sound systems range in complexity and price. At the low end, some two-channel stereo music systems that accept input from your television and VCR can produce a rudimentary form of home theater surround-sound.

The best effects, however, require a dedicated surround-sound system, which features an audio-visual receiver/amplifier; input devices, which can include an audio CD or tape player and a DVD, VCR or laser-disc player; and a full set of speakers. These components can be purchased separately or as a complete system. Prices for surround-sound systems range from a few hundred dollars to several thousand.

A full set of surround-sound speakers includes at least five—one center speaker, two front speakers and two rear speakers. The front speakers produce most of the sound and are typically the best and most expensive in the system. The center speaker carries most of the dialogue and sounds that "move." It should be positioned as close as possible to your television screen, so that dialogue and other central sounds appear to come from the screen itself. Rear speakers handle background sounds, such as applause, traffic noise or the rumble of thunder in the distance.

Some home theater systems also use a subwoofer for very low bass sounds. Because low frequencies are nondirectional, only one subwoofer is needed. The subwoofer is a large speaker that is often hidden under an end table or behind a sofa.

*(above)* **The center speaker** *on a surround-sound system should be positioned near the screen to ensure that movie dialogue sounds authentic.*

*(left)* **Some surround speakers** *can be mounted in a wall or positioned on bookshelves.*

Photo courtesy of Runco International: The World's Finest Home Theater Equipment

*(above)* **A surround-sound** *system with six speakers is crucial to a full-featured home theater. (below left)* **Front-channel speakers** *should usually be positioned just to the sides of the television screen. (below right)* **Good surround-sound speakers** *use a prism shape that effectively distributes sound around the room.*

Photos courtesy of Atlantic Technology International Corp.

# HOME THEATERS

A home theater is the place where all the major electronics come together: large-screen television; stereo VCR, DVD or laser-disc player; and surround-sound system. For many people, a home theater represents the ultimate in home entertainment spaces.

A home theater is where surround-sound really shines. With a movie's sound track filling your room, you become a part of the action. The effect is even greater with a big-screen TV, which adds the visual impression of a full-size movie theater.

Big-screen home theaters are often purchased as a package: projection television, audiovisual receiver, stereo VCR or DVD player, a complete array of surround-sound speakers and a large wall unit to hold the components. The cost for such a full-featured home theater starts at a few thousands dollars, with some versions running into five-digit dollar amounts.

But a fine home theater can also be created with a smaller, more affordable direct-vision television set—perhaps the television set you already own. If your television is at least 27 inches in size and has audiovisual output jacks, it's likely you can create a small home theater simply by adding a few components.

If your television set is a high-end model with a built-in surround-sound amplifier, you may be able to connect additional speakers directly to the television set. It's more likely, however, that you'll need to add an audio-visual receiver/amplifier and to project the television sound track to a set of surround-sound speakers. Surround-sound kits that include the receiver and all necessary speakers are widely available, with prices starting at a few hundred dollars.

When connected to a compatible television, a surround-sound receiver and speakers will give theater sound to any stereo cable or broadcast signal. To get this effect from recorded movies, however, you'll need a DVD player, laser-disc player or a VCR with stereo capability; an older VCR with mono sound doesn't work well in a surround-sound system.

*(above)* **A direct-vision television set** *equipped with a surround-sound receiver and speakers can create a very serviceable home theater. In this example, five surround speakers are integrated into a full-wall storage unit. In a smaller room, this is an excellent option.*

*(opposite)* **A projection television** *lends itself well to a large room with a built-in home theater configuration. In this example, cabinetry conceals the electronic components and speakers.*

To get the best performance from your speakers, proper room placement and mounting are critical. Manufacturers and dealers of surround-sound speakers can provide you with diagrams that show the best speaker arrangements for your space. Knowing the dimensions of your room and the brands and model numbers of your other equipment will help you make the best choices. When you look for surround-sound speakers, take along a drawing of the room that will hold your home theater.

*The electronic components of a large home theater can be conveniently stored in shelving built into a wall. This unit has a wireless remote control unit that controls all elements of the system.*

**Projection televisions** *require that you arrange the room so viewers sit directly in front of the screen. In this home theater, an end table positioned between seats holds a remote control for the ceiling-mounted projection unit. When the theater is not is use, decorative doors hide and protect the screen.*

# HOME THEATERS

(below) **Some home theaters** mimic the look of commerical movie theaters. (bottom) **Family togetherness** gets a boost from a home theater. In this full-featured rec room, a retractable screen can be pulled down for special viewings of favorite family movies and television programs.

**In large rooms,** *surround-sound speakers should be positioned so the sound is clear everywhere in the viewing area. In this home theater, an 80-inch diagonal screen and overhead projection television dominate the room and dictate its style. Remember that projection televisions require a fairly dark room for maximum clarity. This room with plentiful natural light is best suited to nighttime viewing. Daytime viewing of a projection television can be difficult unless you are able to block most of the natural light with heavy drapes.*

# SEATING

One advantage a home theater has over a large commercial theater is comfortable seating. Watching a movie at home from a comfortable couch or recliner is a far more relaxing experience than sitting for two hours in a stiff theater seat penned in by other patrons.

Whether you plan to use it for listening to music or watching television, you'll spend most of the time in your home entertainment area sitting down. That's why choosing the right seating can be as important as selecting your electronic components.

Your choices for home theater seating are almost unlimited, but the most popular selections include sofas, love seats, sectionals, recliners and armchairs with ottomans. These basic pieces are available in so many styles that it's usually easy to find comfortable selections to match your decorating scheme. For maximum relaxation, consider buying orthopedically designed chairs or recliners.

Custom seating for home theaters may be the best choice for serious movie buffs, audiophiles or big-screen sports fans. These specially designed chairs and modular sections can be used alone or put together in combinations. Some even have heat and massage options, hidden drink trays and remote-control compartments.

*Side-by-side recliner units* simulate the atmosphere of a commercial movie theater, but in unique comfort. This triple seating unit has pop-up footrests and built-in beverage holders. Scaled-down versions of this type of seating are available for children (above).

**Traditional movie theater seats** *are now available for home theaters, making the viewing experience truly authentic. They can be special-ordered individually, or in rows to match a room of any size (bottom).*

# PARLOR GAMES

Parlor games played by civilized contestants sitting around a table have been a staple of home entertainment spaces for thousands of years. Parlor games are welcome and easily added features for any entertainment area, and they lend a timeless atmosphere to the space. Chess, checkers, Mah-jongg and many card games still popular today have their origins many hundreds of years in the past. All you really need to enjoy a fun board game or hand of cards is a tabletop large enough for players to sit around comfortably and adequate light over the table. Folding card tables are an easy way to add parlor games to an area without permanently losing any valuable floor space.

In a room devoted to parlor games, traffic flow can be important. The furniture you choose should allow everyone to move about the room freely and should be arranged to help direct traffic flow. Gaming tables with reversible tops offer a greater variety of possibilities, and some bumper pool tables can

be converted for use as tables for cards and board games.

Good overhead lighting is important in entertainment areas where parlor games are a popular activity. The lighting you choose also contributes to the ambience of the room. Consider decorative hanging lamps with stained glass designs that add an old-fashioned flavor to a gaming parlor. Chairs that roll on casters are useful, especially in areas that get heavy traffic. Casters allow people to roll out of the way whenever necessary.

In larger groups and playing longer games, you and your guests will probably get hungry and thirsty. If you have space set aside in your home entertainment area for preparing food and drinks, the action doesn't have to stop. You may simply want to add a microwave oven for heating up snacks and a small refrigerator for keeping drinks cool. Cleaning up will also be easier if you install a sink or if your home entertainment area is near the kitchen.

*This octagonal backgammon table* doubles as a snack and cocktail table. Matching bar stools contribute to the tavern atmosphere.

(left) **This casino table** has a felt surface and slots for holding poker chips and drinks. It is styled for poker but can also be used for bridge and other card games. Armchairs mounted on rolling casters add comfort to the gaming experience.

(below) **The classic Carrom game board** originated in the 1890s. More than 93 games can be played on both sides of the board, including ring billiards, checkers and backgammon. At minimal cost, a Carrom board can provide hundreds of hours of fun for the whole family.

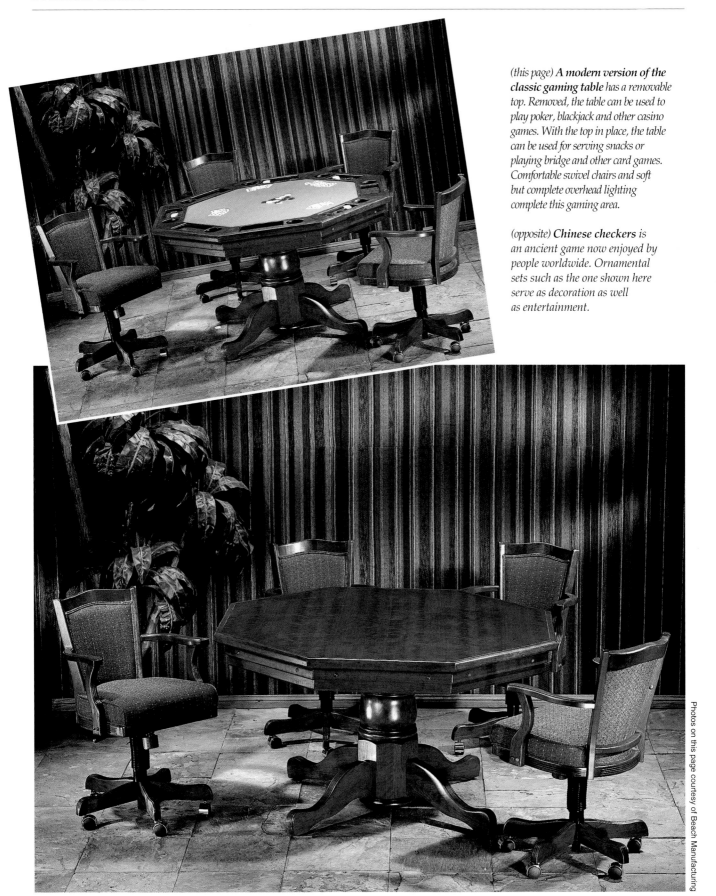

(this page) **A modern version of the classic gaming table** has a removable top. Removed, the table can be used to play poker, blackjack and other casino games. With the top in place, the table can be used for serving snacks or playing bridge and other card games. Comfortable swivel chairs and soft but complete overhead lighting complete this gaming area.

(opposite) **Chinese checkers** is an ancient game now enjoyed by people worldwide. Ornamental sets such as the one shown here serve as decoration as well as entertainment.

Photo courtesy of Bartley Antique Reproduction Furniture Kits

(opposite) *A fine backgammon set* with inlaid woods lends an elegant tone to a gaming room.

(right) *A fine end table with* an inlaid chess board is a perfect addition to a formal gaming room. This table has offset sides that can be used to hold drinks and snacks—or a timer's clock, for competitive chess players.

(below) *Chess sets* are available in many styles with pieces depicting different historical conflicts. In this set, the figures depict characters from ancient Egyptian history and mythology.

This and opposite photo courtesy of The Franklin Mint

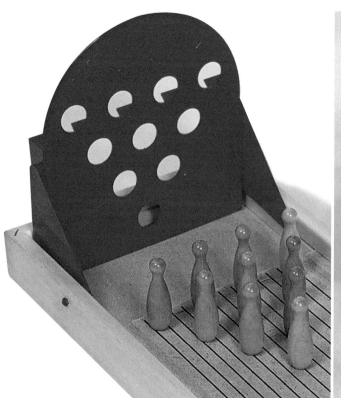
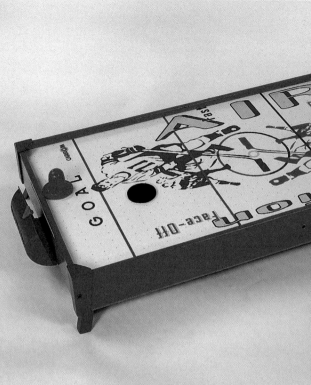

# INDOOR SPORTS

In addition to parlor games, which are mostly mental, your entertainment space can also be home to more physical sporting games. Sports designed for indoor play include table tennis, billiards and darts. You can also include simulation versions of outdoor games: table soccer and air hockey, for example.

As you can imagine, space can be a limiting factor in your decision to include indoor sports. Billiards tables are among the most difficult items to fit into an entertainment area. The minimum space required to play on the smallest standard table size, using a 57-inch cue stick, is 12½ ft. × 15 ft.

Similarly, Ping-Pong® tables take up a lot of space—17 ft. × 19 ft. for a regulation 5 ft. × 9 ft. table. However, many models feature wheels and can be folded up in the middle when not in use.

If you have a hard time deciding between table tennis and billiards, or would like both games, special tabletops are available for converting a pool table into a Ping-Pong table. For a reasonable cost, you can enjoy both indoor sports.

FREE THROW DUEL

GOAL

FOUL

Photos courtesy of Carrom Company

*(above right)* **Free-throw duel** *provides lots of action, but collapses for easy storage once the competition is over.*

*(above left)* **Air hockey** *is popular with young and old alike. This tabletop version can be stored in a closet or left out to provide a colorful diversion for children.*

*(left)* **This miniature bowling game** *is just four feet long and can fit nicely on an ordinary card table. It's a favorite among kids.*

45

# AIR HOCKEY & TABLE SOCCER

If you like active indoor sports but don't have quite enough room for a billiards table or Ping-Pong® table, air hockey and table soccer are good options.

Air hockey, also called table hockey, is played on a vinyl-clad table six or seven feet long. Air hockey tables weight less than 200 pounds, so they can be moved by two or three people to make space for other activities without too much trouble.

Table soccer units are about five feet wide, including the handles, and six feet long. You'll need a space about 10 ft. square to comfortably accommodate four players. Table soccer units weigh between 200 and 250 pounds.

If noise is one of your concerns, you'll want to be sure these games are away from sleeping areas.

**Table soccer games**, *first popular on college campuses and in arcades, are now found in many home entertainment rooms.*

Photos courtesy of Carrom Company

*(above)* **Tabletop air hockey games** *are about four feet long and can be easily set up and stored.*

*(left)* **This floor-standing air hockey game** *is seven feet long and has a battery-operated electronic scoring feature. This model can be folded up for storage. Children love the noise and action of air hockey.*

# DARTS

The game of darts originated centuries ago in Europe, when soldiers would pass the time hurling short spears at cross sections of logs. Over the years, the equipment has evolved into soft-tipped darts and electronic boards, but dart throwing has remained one of the most popular indoor games in the country.

The easiest way to set up a dart room in your home is with a prepackaged game that comes complete and ready to play. Most packages include a dart board, a 9-volt power pack, six high-quality darts, extra dart tips, mounting hardware and an instruction manual. Because options vary from board to board, look for one that allows as many as four players to play at one time, as well as one player alone against the computer. Most electronic dart boards are preprogrammed with a number of games and extra features, some with as many as 17 games for up to four players.

The game of darts requires ample, convenient seating for players and observers. Tall stools and tables are nice because they make it easier for players to stand up and sit down between turns.

Good light over the dart board is essential, and can be achieved with a hanging ceiling fixture, directed track lights or a recessed ceiling light.

You'll need storage spaces to keep darts and accessories. You might also want to find some way to enclose the board so it can be kept out of sight. Many attractive cabinets are available, designed specifically to house a dart board, darts and tips, and other miscellaneous items.

Photo courtesy of IKEA

(left) **Modern dart boards** use safe, plastic-tipped darts and feature electronic sensors to keep score automatically for up to four players. Expansion memory cartridges that plug into the board offer dozens of different game variations.

(opposite) **Dart boards** are not always used in a regulation setting. Often they are tucked in the corner of a child's bedroom.

# BILLIARDS

"Billiards" is a term used to refer to any game played with billiard balls and cue sticks on a table, with or without pockets. The familiar billiard table most people recognize is designed for a game called "pocket pool." If you are considering a pocket pool table for your entertainment area, it will be important for you to evaluate the room size first.

Pool tables come in four standard sizes. The amount of room needed for comfortable pool playing depends on the size of the table and the length of the cue stick you use. Cue sticks come in three standard lengths: 48", 52" and 57". The chart on the opposite page can help you determine if your entertainment area has sufficient room for a pocket pool table.

A billiards option for smaller spaces is a bumper pool table, which measures about 4 feet in diameter. In addition to being great fun for bumper pool, some tables have tops that convert them into parlor-style gaming tables. This adds versatility to the space by offering an entertainment area that can be used either for pool or for table games, such as cards, chess and cribbage.

The best billiards tables are made from single pieces of slate for flatness and true ball roll. They are covered with high-quality billiard cloth, which allows smooth play and wears well. Table designs range from traditional large, handsome wood tables to contemporary models of black laminate with chrome corners and matching trim, which have a sleek, modern look.

Photo courtesy of Brunswick Billiards

*For the best gaming experience, equip your billiards room with a 4½' × 9' table and use 57" cue sticks. Such a set requires a large space, however—at least 14' × 18' in size. Such professional tables feature 1"-thick solid slate beds and can weigh well over a thousand pounds. Before choosing such a table, make sure your floors can tolerate this weight.*

## Ideal Room Size: Per Table by Cue Length

| TABLE SIZE (PLAYING SURFACE) | 48" CUES | 52" CUES | 57" CUES |
|---|---|---|---|
| 3.5' x 7' (39" x 78") | 11'3" x 14'6" | 11'11' x 15'2" | 12'9" x 16'0" |
| 4' x 8' (44" x 88") | 11'8" x 15'4" | 12'4" x 16'0 | 13'2" x16'10" |
| 4' x 8' OS (46" x 92") | 12' x 15'8" | 12'6" x 16'4" | 13'4" x 17'2" |
| 4.5' x 9' (50" x 100") | 12'2" x 16'4" | 12'10" x 17'0" | 13'8" x 17'10" |

*By far the most popular size table for the home is 4'x 8', and the standard cue length is 57".*

*(above)* **The smallest pocket pool tables** *are 3' × 6' models. When 48" cue sticks are used, you can fit a small pool table in a space about 10' ×13' in size.*

*(left)* **Bumper pool tables** *offer different types of billiards games and require less space than pocket pool tables.*

51

Lighting for areas with pool tables should include hanging lights over the table for shadowless illumination. You can establish a traditional pool parlor theme by using decorative light fixtures.

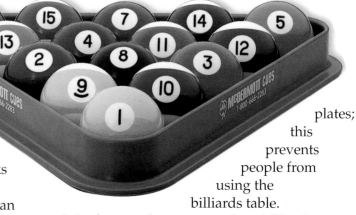

Pool cues themselves are aesthetically pleasing in appearance; a handsome display rack can both provide storage for your cue sticks and serve as an artistic accent.

A billiards area may have stools so players can easily stand up and sit down during the course of a game, and additional seating can be helpful for spectators. It's also important to include a table, bar or countertop surface for resting drinks and plates; this prevents people from using the billiards table.

It is always advantageous for a billiards room to have well-insulated walls; the sharp crack of pool balls rebounding off one another can travel and be quite loud.

# VIRTUAL GOLF

Some of the newest sporting games for home use are indoor golf units. You can find putting greens that electronically reconfigure the slope and angle of the "green" in dozens of different contours. Thus, you can play a variety of holes with one machine, helping you develop your skill at gauging speed, direction and break. Ball return is automatic, and a computer tracks scores, total strokes and average putts per hole for as many as four people at a time. With this type of putting equipment, a whole family can enjoy a game of mini-golf. Putting greens can be set up in minutes and folded away for easy storage.

You can also find driving machines that can compute your drive distance and tell you whether your drive hooked, sliced or went straight. These machines can be used indoors or out—you just need enough room to swing a golf club (high ceilings are helpful). Driving machines can be adjusted to three height options— teed high, teed low or a fairway lie. You can choose from six club options and can easily configure the machine for left-handed swings.

For serious golfers, there are new automatic driving ranges that tee up balls, catch your drives at full velocity in an all-weather net and shag them back to the tee.

*(right) **Virtual putting games** challenge the golfer by changing the pitch and slope of each putt.*

*(opposite) **A complete billiards area** will have one or more overhanging light fixtures for even illumination and a wall rack for storing cue sticks and other accessories.*

Photo courtesy of The Sharper Image

# FOOD & BEVERAGE SERVICE

The point of creating any home entertainment area is to enjoy the time you spend in it, and refreshments can play a big part of that enjoyment. Almost any entertainment space is improved by adding provisions for storing and preparing snacks.

For small entertainment spaces used just for your immediate family, a small refrigerator for beverages and a popcorn maker may be all you need. Adding a small microwave oven and a storage cabinet for snacks makes your space more versatile.

For large recreation spaces where you regularly entertain visitors, you may want to include a full wet bar and possibly even a small stove and dishwasher.

Your food and drink choices will vary depending on your preferences, activities and the time of day. Snack crackers and dip, pretzels and nuts, and soft drinks go well with afternoon games and television events; for evening parlor games or indoor sports matches, sandwiches and soft drinks or beer provide a pleasant break from the action; your late night gatherings may call for coffee and dessert. If you enjoy mixed drinks, consider installing a full wet bar with plumbing and a drain, plus a blender for making favorite

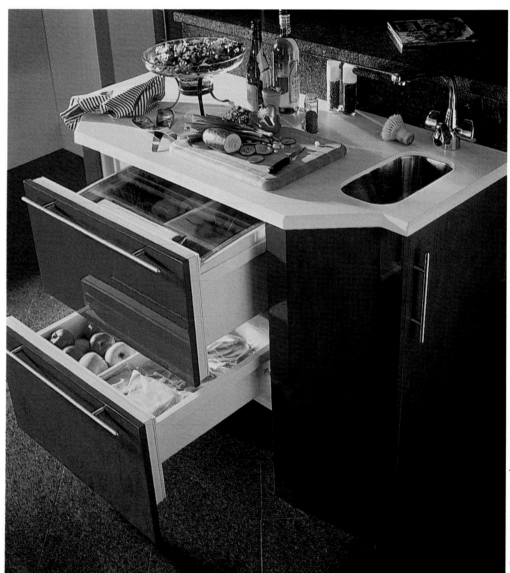

*(right) This **small snack station** includes built-in refrigerator shelves and a small bar sink, yet occupies less than ten square feet of floor space.*

*(opposite) **This wet bar** mimics the look of a classic movie theater snack bar. It is an ideal addition for a home theater space.*

Photo courtesy of Sub-Zero Freezer Co., Inc.

iced drinks like margaritas and daiquiris.

If you have space for the equipment and use your entertainment area often, convenience alone may be reason enough to include a place to prepare food and drinks. From the most basic pieces, such as a small refrigerator and microwave oven, to the most specialized, such as an espresso maker or a wine captain, think first about your needs. Then have fun setting up your food and beverage service area.

Photo courtesy of Exposures Catalog

(above right) **This "wine-taster's table"** is a historical reproduction that features a polished marble tabletop and two built-in ice buckets for holding chilled wine. Drawers can be used to store accessories, and the lower shelf can hold stemware.

(right) **This wet bar and snack preparation area** includes a low-profile refrigerator installed under the counter. The refrigerator opens to the front of the bar for easy access.

Photo courtesy of Sub-Zero Freezer Co., Inc.

*(top, left)* **Soda chargers** *let you enjoy sparkling water and other carbonated beverages. They are ideal for making cocktails, wine spritzers and flavored seltzer waters.*

*(top, center)* **A cocktail shaker** *is traditionally used for mixing and chilling cocktails with crushed ice. This style can be monogrammed for a personal touch.*

*(top, right)* **A butler table** *lets you serve snacks and beverages with a touch of elegance.*

*(left)* **A decorative bar cabinet** *holds fine liquors and stemware in style.*

# A PORTFOLIO OF

# HOME
# ENTERTAINMENT
## IDEAS

*Comfortable furniture, soft, indirect lighting and elegant storage* make a home listening area a truly relaxing space. In the room shown here, the modern shelving unit has a semitransparent sliding door that hides the stereo components.

Photo courtesy of interlübke

Above right photo courtesy NSM America

# HOME LISTENING AREAS

Home listening areas are most attractive to people who take music appreciation very seriously. These are areas where your favorite music can flourish in a great environment. Large or small rooms can be used to create your personal home listening area. You can choose a simple, low-key approach with a minimalist feel, or you may decide to take a more elegant approach, creating a listening area with sculpted carpet, leather upholstery and rich fabrics on the walls.

Furniture in home listening areas should be comfortable and relaxing. Soft, diffused lighting, natural fibers and a balance between hard and soft surfaces in the room all help you control sound distribution. Remember that hard surfaces reflect sound, so a powerful system might sound muddy if sound is reflected by too many surfaces in a room. On the other hand, if a room has mostly soft surfaces, sound can be absorbed and become lost.

Cabinetry can both store and display stereo equipment and other components. A beautiful custom cabinet is an ideal choice for the centerpiece of your home entertainment area.

*(above)* **Ultramodern sound equipment** *complements the stark, sleek decor of this attic getaway.*

*(left)* **Plastic "hold everything" tubes** *can be used to organize and protect all the wires running from stereos and other electronic equipment.*

Photo courtesy of Hold Everything, photography by Stefano Massei
Above photo courtesy of Meridian America Inc.

*(above)* **Rugs, throw pillows and wall hangings** *can absorb sound and minimize echo in rooms with bare ceramic or wood floors.*

*(right)* **Storage containers** *can be decorative as well as functional. These attractive wicker boxes are ideal for storing CDs, remote controls and other small accessories.*

Photo courtesy of Hold Everything, photography by Stefano Massei
Above photo courtesy of Meridian America Inc.

63

Photo courtesy of interlübke

*A bedroom* doubles as a home
listening center when a compact
component stereo system is integrated
into a headboard storage unit. With a
small chair and flexible lighting, even
a small bedroom can be used as an
intimate, multifunction entertainment
space for reading and listening to music.

*Modular shelving and storage units* allow you to alter configurations to suit changing needs. A wide variety of modular systems are available, in styles ranging from ultramodern to elegant traditional. Modular systems are especially useful for apartment dwellers, for whom built-in systems are not practical.

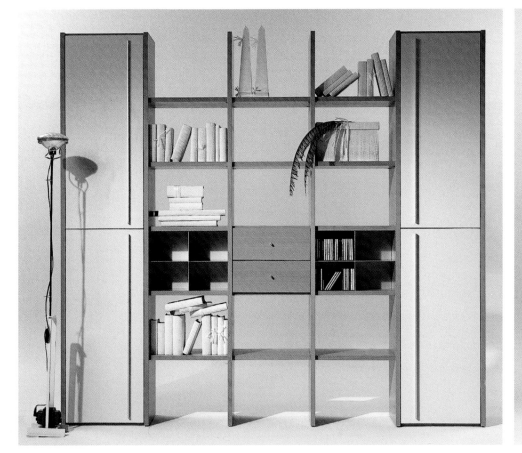

(right) **This jukebox** featuring peacocks is decorated with six bubble tubes, rotating colors in the side column and incredible "polarization of light" in which every feather in the peacock plumes changes color independently from feather to feather.

(below) **Art deco fawns** playing the Pipes of Pan above two leaping gazelles etched in mirrored glass panels make this classic jukebox a collector's item. The gazelles are brilliantly illuminated with ever-changing colors. The classic craftsmanship includes carved walnut and alder hardwoods.

*A jukebox gives a room a classic tavern feel, and the warm, luminous light provides atmosphere. Modern jukeboxes come equipped with SyberSonic™ electronics. An Intel® processor drives the prime features: dual amplifiers with surround-sound, remote controls and multiple languages, all at the touch of a button.*

***Today's theater*** with a big-screen projection television, plush seating and indirect mood lighting can virtually duplicate the commercial movie theater experience. A spacious basement rec room is an ideal place to create such a home theater.

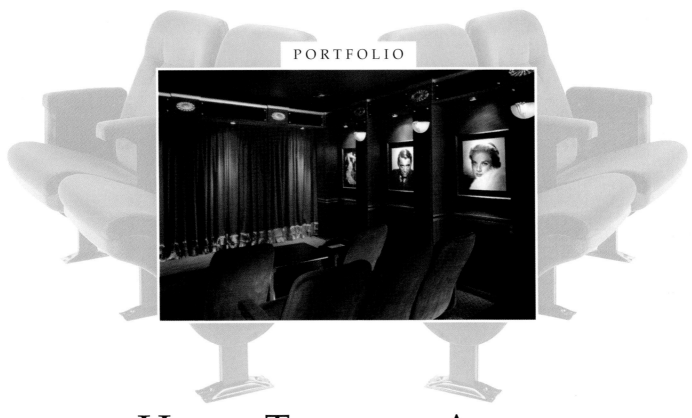

# HOME THEATER AREAS

Imagine yourself sinking deep into the plush, deep cushions of a sectional couch or settling into a fancy theater-style seat. The walls are adorned with larger-than-life posters of movie stars from yesterday and today. You are ready to be transported away to a distant land or even to another galaxy. An engaging home theater will take you almost anywhere you want to go.

A home theater adds drama and presence to any viewing experience. Modern home theaters can create a remarkably realistic atmosphere, complete with theater seating, movie-related decor and popcorn makers. The theater-style furniture currently available includes custom rockers and recliners, some with built-in armrests and beverage holders. More conventional home theaters feature multipiece sectional couches with deep cushions, footstools and lots of extra pillows.

Many home theater areas are designed to keep the big-screen out of sight when it's not being used. A big-screen television is often shut away inside a cabinet behind closed doors, or the screen for a projection TV is hidden in a wall or ceiling. When you want to enjoy a theater atmosphere, you simply open the cabinet or pull out the projection screen for viewing.

For maximum enjoyment, many people equip their home theaters with the largest screens possible. Screens larger than 35 inches will most likely be front or rear projection screens. Remember that larger screens require a greater viewing distance for comfortable viewing. The screens for front projection units may use a retractable pull-down design, or they may be mounted flush against a wall. The screen often takes center stage in a wall system designed to hold all the elements of a home theater.

Other elements also enhance your enjoyment of a home theater area. All the seating for a home theater should offer a comfortable view of the screen, and you should have ample room for people to move around as they need. Surround-sound speakers that blend into the aesthetics of the room provide the feeling of movie theater sound without detracting from the atmosphere.

***Modern home theater components*** *can be
integrated into the most traditional of decorating
schemes. In this elegant formal living room, the
electronic components are stored in stylish built-in
shelving, and the viewing screen can be pulled
down or retracted at will.*

*A small home theater* can be contained in a single cabinet. In the configuration shown here, decorative sliding panels on the shelving unit open to reveal a small but full-featured home theater station. Subdued lighting and a comfortable armchair with ottoman complete the room.

Photos this page courtesy of Milling Road, A Division of Baker Furniture

*(above and opposite) **A wide variety of armoire-style cabinets** are available to store complete home theater centers. Many are large enough to also hold a complete array of stereo equipment. Better cabinets have doors that can be retracted, an extendable rotating platform for the television, and compartmentalized storage for a VCR, stereo receiver, videotapes, CDs and other accessories. Such cabinets are ideal for a home theater located in a bedroom.*

***Classic board games,*** *like chess, checkers and Mah-jongg have been the focal points of gaming rooms for many centuries. In this traditional-style gaming room, game pieces, furniture, lighting and decorations have been carefully selected to create a historical mood.*

# AREAS FOR
# INDOOR SPORTS & GAMES

Home entertainment spaces dedicated to parlor games and indoor sports generally take their style cues from the types of games played there. If you play classic board games, like chess and checkers, a classic room style with a mature and sophisticated atmosphere and moody lighting might be appropriate. A room devoted to card games or billiards might call for dark woods, rich colors and decorative overhead light fixtures, reproducing the ambience of a traditional gaming parlor. A room used for table soccer or pinball, on the other hand, naturally calls

for bright lighting and a more high-tech decor.

When designing the look of your indoor sports and game room, you will be able to choose from a variety of design styles, from traditional to ultramodern, from minimalist to audaciously extravagant. Whatever style you choose, try to find one special element that provides a focal point and gives voice to the atmosphere you seek. In a 1950s style game room, for example, a jukebox or soda fountain might be the crowning touch. In a billiards room, an antique hanging light fixture with stained glass can establish the mood and focus.

*A gaming table with an inlaid grid surface* is a classic furniture choice for gaming rooms. Most tables have a drawer to safely store gaming pieces and can also be used as end tables for serving snacks.

***Checkers game board*** *is painted on the wood floor in a corner of the family room. Floor pillows are used for comfortable seating while playing checkers.*

*A **set of chess pieces** can be a work of art that helps set the tone for your gaming room. Highly prized as collectors' items, chess sets can be made from rare hardwoods, stainless steel, pewter, marble, granite—even jade or turquoise. Styles often mimic notable historical conflicts: North vs. South in the Civil War; British vs. the Colonies during the American Revolution; Robin Hood vs. the Sheriff of Nottingham. The chess set shown here honors the royal houses of medieval China and Japan.*

*(right)* **Finely crafted cue sticks** *made from rare hardwoods can serve a decorative as well as functional purpose.*

*(below)* **A billiards table,** *by virtue of its sheer size, is generally the centerpiece of a gaming room. In addition to its sporting function, a billiards table can serve as decorative furniture. Tables are available in many styles, finishes and wood types. A green felt tabletop surface is traditional, but red, gray and blue surfaces are also available.*

*(opposite)* **Billiards and card tables** *placed by windows or in unexpected rooms give an altogether different feel to your entertainment area.*

This and above photo courtesy of Cal Spas

Photo courtesy of Valley Recreation Products

Photo courtesy of Cowles Creative Publishing, Inc.
Opposite photo of pool cues courtesy of McDERMOTT Cue Mfg., Inc.

**Loyal sports fans** *can give gaming rooms a strong theme by choosing furnishings and accessories embellished with the trademarks of their favorite teams. Some manufacturers of gaming tables, for example, let you choose from a wide variety of sports team logos at purchase time. To complete the effect, you can choose floorcoverings, draperies, wall decorations and dishes that use the team colors or designs.*

*Clever use of space* is important for a multifunction entertainment space. A complete entertainment area can provide space for storage and preparation of snacks and beverages. The room shown here features a refrigerated drawer unit built into a wall shelving unit, perfect for chilling wines and soft drinks.

Photo courtesy of Sub-Zero Freezer Co., Inc.

Above right photo courtesy of Broyhill Furniture Industries, Inc.

# MULTIFUNCTIONAL
# HOME ENTERTAINMENT AREAS

Many home entertainment spaces focus on one or two types of activities, but if you're lucky enough to have a large space—a spacious basement not yet used for other functions, for example—you may be able to create a multi-functional entertainment center that holds a variety of popular indoor sports and games, with tables and chairs for playing parlor games, and the latest in video games, pinball machines, bumper pool and table soccer. Some multi-functional areas are large enough to include all these, plus a full-size billiards table and a complete home theater system.

Of course, you won't always be able to include all these elements in a single home entertainment space. But through creative use of space and proper choice of elements, even smaller entertainment spaces can include several different activities. The ideas on the following pages will show you ways this can be accomplished.

(this page) **Storage is** important to any recreation space, but it's especially crucial for multifunction areas that contain a wide selection of electronic equipment, books, CDs, videotapes, games and accessories.

(opposite) **Modular cabinets and shelving units** offer a good way to build your multifunction entertainment space a little at a time. Open floor-to-ceiling shelves can hold books and decorative pieces, while door and drawer cabinets can hold electronics and other items.

*(right)* **Downsized furniture** *and components will allow you to fit many elements into a room. This steel and glass storage unit holds just as many components and accessories as a full, wall-size storage unit made from wood.*

*(below)* **Entertainment spaces** *can provide for active as well as passive recreation. This room is designed for musical performance as well as for listening. Attractive mood lighting and furnishings also make this an ideal space for reading and other forms of relaxation.*

**The heart of a multifunctional** entertainment space is a flexible, expandable storage scheme. Here, an open modular shelving system can be reconfigured whenever new elements are added, or whenever a new look is desired. Open shelving of this type creates an airy, spacious tone that is well suited to informal, modern decorating styles.

# PORTFOLIO

*(right) **Ice buckets, coasters, cocktail glasses and bar utensils** make attractive, functional accessories.*

*(below) **Built-in appliances** for food storage and preparation are welcome additions to almost any entertainment space. A small bar sink and an undercabinet refrigerator with pull-out drawers take up little space, but add enormous convenience.*

*(opposite) **Stock kitchen cabinetry** can be used to create a versatile wet bar and food preparation center in a recreation space.*

Photo courtesy of Kraftware Corporation

Photo courtesy of Sub-Zero Freezer Co., Inc.

*Traditional armoire-style cabinets* are specially designed to hold home entertainment equipment in style. Used in a bedroom (left) or living room (below), this type of cabinet elegantly conceals the components when not in use, but provides a full-featured home entertainment center whenever you want it. Armoire-style cabinets are ideal for any room with a traditional decorating scheme, where high-tech electronic equipment clashes with the other furnishings.

# LIST OF CONTRIBUTORS

We'd like to thank the following companies for providing the photographs used in this book:

Abbacus, Inc.
1248 Shapport Drive
Machesnry Park, IL 61115
(800) 988-4261

Artemide Inc.
1980 New Highway
Farmingdale, NY 11735
(516) 694-9292

Atlantic Technology
International Corp.
343 Vanderbilt Avenue
Norwood, MA 02062
(781) 762-6300

Audio Design Associates, Inc.
602-610 Mamaroneck Avenue
White Plains, NY 10605
(800) 43-AUDIO

Axcess Marketing/
LOVAN Audio
1306 Kingsdale Avenue
Redondo Beach, CA 90278
(310) 793-7676

Bartley Antique Reproduction
Furniture Kits
65 Engerman Avenue
Denton, MD 21629
(410) 479-4480

Bauer International, Inc.
414 Jessen Lane
Wando, SC 29492
(803) 884-4007

Beach Manufacturing
13872 West Street
Garden Grove, CA 92843
(714) 265-3680

Broyhill Furniture
Industries, Inc.
One Broyhill Park
Lenoir, NC 28633-0001
(704) 758-3111

Brunswick Billiards
8663 196th Avenue
Bristol, WI 53104
(800) 336-8764

Cal Spas
1462 East Ninth Street
Pomona, CA 91766
(909) 623-8781

Carrom Company
PO Box 649,
215 East Dowland Street
Ludington, MI 49431-0649
(616) 843-9276

Drexel Heritage
Furnishings, Inc.
101 North Main Street
Drexel, NC 28619
(800) 916-1986

Exposures Catalog
27 Ann Street
South Norwalk, CT 06854
(203) 854-1610

First Impressions Design &
Management, Inc.
12564 N.E. 14th Avenue
N. Miami, FL 33161
(800) 305-7545

The Franklin Mint
U.S. Route 1, West Stow Road
Franklin Center, PA 19091
(610) 459-6000

Hold Everything
PO Box 7807
San Francisco, CA 94120-7807
(800) 421-2264

IKEA
496 West Germantown Pike
Plymouth Meeting, PA 19462
East Coast: (410) 931-8940
West Coast: (818) 912-1119

interlübke
PO Box 139
Athens, NY 12015
(518) 945-1007

Irwin Seating Company, Inc.
Home Theater Division
165 City View Drive
Etobicoke, Ontario M9W 5B1
(905) 820-6577

KraftMaid Cabinetry, Inc.
15535 South State Avenue,
PO Box 1055
Middlefield, OH 44062
(800) 571-1990

Kraftware Corporation
675 Garfield Avenue
Jersey City, NJ 07305
(201) 434-4200
(800) 221-1728 (Outside NJ)

McDERMOTT Cue Mfg., Inc.
W146 N9560 Held Drive
Menomonee Falls, WI 53051
(800) 666-2283

Meridian America Inc.
3800 Camp Creek Parkway,
Building 2400, Suite 112
Atlanta, GA 30331
(404) 344-7111

Merillat Industries, Inc.
PO Box 1946
Adrian, MI 49221
(517) 263-0771

Milling Road,
A Division of Baker Furniture
329 North Hamilton
High Point, NC 27260
(336) 885-1800

Niles Audio Corporation, Inc.
12331 S.W. 130th Street
Miami, FL 33186
(305) 238-4373

NSM America
1158 Tower Lane
Benserville, IL 60106
(630) 860-5100

Olhausen Billiard
Manufacturing, Inc.
12460 Kirkham Court
Poway, CA 92064
(800) 866-4606

Paul M. Berg Photography
405 Coloma Street
Sausalito, CA 94965
(415) 332-2226

Roche-Bobois
183 Madison Avenue
New York, NY 10016
(800) 972-8375

ROCK-OLA® Mfg. Corporation
2335 208th Street
Torrance, CA 90501
(310) 328-1306

Room & Board
4600 Olson Memorial Highway
Minneapolis, MN 55422
(800) 486-6554

Runco International
2463 Tripaldi Way
Hayward, CA 99545
(510) 293-9154

The Sharper Image
650 Davis Street
San Francisco, CA 94111
(800) 344-4444

Sub-Zero Freezer Co., Inc.
4717 Hammersley Road
Madison, WI 53711
(608) 271-2233

Techline Furniture
500 S. Division Street
Waunakee, WI 53597
(800) 356-8400

U. Schaerer Sons Inc./
HALLER SYSTEMS™
150 East 58th Street
New York, NY 10155
(212) 371-1230

Valley Recreation Products
333 Morton Street
Bay City, MI 48706
(517) 892-4536

Vidikron
One Evertrust Plaza,
11th Floor
Jersey City, NJ 07302
(800) VID-KRON

Williams-Sonoma
PO Box 7456
San Francisco, CA
94120-7456
(800) 541-2233